Disney LEARNING

Where Do Animals Live?

pi kids®

phoenix international publications, inc.

Animals from all over the savanna gather to see Simba, their future king! A savanna is a grassland that is hot and dry. Savannas have a lot of different grasses, but just a few trees. Every animal needs water—so every animal on the savanna knows where the waterholes are.

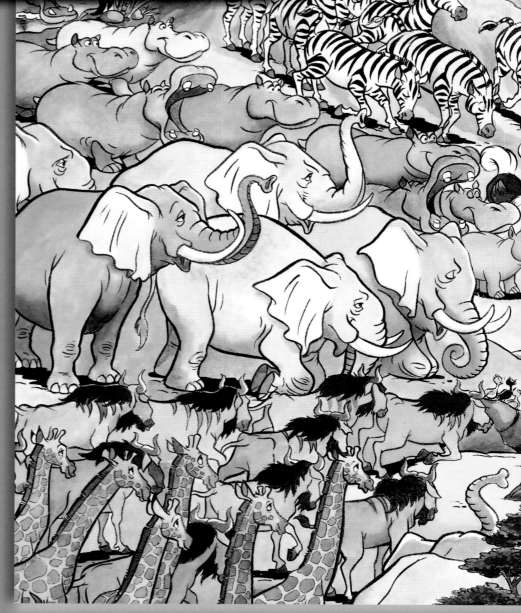

Find Zazu.
Red-billed hornbills like Zazu eat bugs. Look for birds and bugs near your home and draw them.

Find this hippo.
A hippo baby can ride on its mother's back while she swims. How do humans travel with babies?

Find this cheetah.
Cheetahs can run up to 70 miles per hour. How fast can you run? Pick a start and finish line and ask someone to time you.

Find Nala.
Lion families work together to hunt. How does your family work together to buy food, prepare it, and clean up? Make badges showing who does what job.

Find Shenzi, Banzai, and Ed.
Hyenas live in caves, which keep them cool, dry, and safe. Draw your home. Label the parts that keep you safe and comfortable.

Match these photos of savanna animals to their partners in the Pride Lands:

Pocahontas shows John Smith that the forest is full of wonder. Temperate forests have warm summers and cool or cold winters. They get a lot of rain or snow. Most trees in the temperate forest lose their leaves in the fall and grow them back in the spring.

Find the hummingbird.

A flying hummingbird's heart can beat up to 1,200 beats per minute! Human heartbeats are much slower. Get an adult to help you take your pulse.

Find the fox.

Foxes appear in many folktales as cunning, clever characters. Make up a story starring a fox.

Find the rattlesnake.

Rattlesnake rattles are actually dry rings of skin hitting against each other. Make a rattle: put some dried beans in a paper cup or bag and shake.

Find this bear cub.

Bears have a keen sense of smell. Plug your nose and eat a piece of apple and a piece of potato. Without smell, how do they compare?

Find the blue jay.

Blue jays sometimes help plants grow by hiding seeds and nuts and then forgetting to come back for them. Plant a seed and watch it sprout.

Match these photos of forest animals to their partners in the Virginia wilderness:

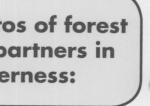

There are plenty of fish in the river for Merida and her Mother-Bear to catch! When rain, springwater, or melted snow or ice flow down a slope, a stream is formed. This stream joins other streams to become a river. The river eventually empties out to an ocean or sea.

Find this salmon.

Salmon are born in rivers and swim to the sea as adults. Later, they return to where they were born. Describe your earliest memory of your home.

Find the beehive.

Honeybees make beeswax to build their homes. Look at the outside of your home. List the materials you see, such as wood, brick, or aluminum.

Find the web.

Spiders can "read" vibrations on their web. Stretch a rubber band between your fingers and pluck it. Can you feel the vibrations? Can you hear them?

Find this dragonfly.

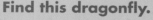

Dragonfly adults live near water. Dragonfly babies live underwater. Make a list of traits you have in common with an adult and a list of traits that differ.

Find the nest.

A bird might build its home in spaces between rocks. Find a crack in the sidewalk or between fence posts. Draw plants and insects you see there.

Match these photos of river animals to their homes near Merida's river:

Dory and friends play hide-and-seek in their coral reef home. A coral reef is a colorful colony of living and dead coral. Coral reefs are found in warm, shallow parts of the ocean. Many different species of coral form a reef, and that reef hosts plants and sea animals of all types.

Find Sheldon.

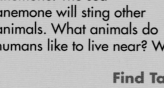

A seahorse holds onto things with its tail, like a hand. Try holding things without using your hands. How can you use your arms? Your feet?

Find Nemo.

A clownfish stays safe by living near a sea anemone. The sea anemone will sting other animals. What animals do humans like to live near? Why?

Find Tad.

A butterfly fish is round and flat, like a pancake. Draw a funny picture of a pancake-fish. Draw other animals with shapes or colors that remind you of different objects.

Find Hank.

Octopuses have brain cells in their arms as well as their brains! Split your brain's focus: try rubbing your belly and patting your head at the same time.

Find Destiny.

A whale shark like Destiny can be 50 times longer than a blue tang like Dory. Measure the height of everyone in your family, including pets. Who is tallest? Shortest?

Match these photos of marine animals to their partners on Nemo's reef:

Carl and Russell rest on a tepui after their long day looking for Paradise Falls. Shaped like a table top, a tepui is a special kind of mountain in Venezuela. Many of the plants and animals living on the tepui are different from the plants and animals in the jungle far below.

Find the bat.

Bats *echolocate* (use sound vibrations) to get around. Ask permission to test different spots in a gym or auditorium for the best echo. Make a map showing your findings.

Find the mouse opossum.

Mouse opossums can climb very well. Set a climbing goal for yourself, such as going down a tall slide or swinging across the monkey bars.

Find the anteater.

Anteaters have thick fur to protect against biting ants. How do your clothes and shoes protect you from sun? Cold? Cuts and scrapes?

Find the capybara.

Capybaras must live near water in order to stay healthy. Keep track of how many times a day you use water, and in what ways.

Find the jaguar.

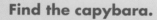

Jaguars are fierce predators. Their name means "he who kills with one leap" in the Guaraní language. How did you get your name? What meaning does it have?

Match these photos of tepui animals to their partners around Russell and Carl's campfire:

Tiana, Naveen, and their new friends make their musical way to Mama Odie's bayou. A bayou, or swamp, is a place where the ground is covered with shallow water. Swamps form near rivers and coastlines. A swamp is similar to a marsh. The main difference is that swamps have trees and marshes have grasses.

Find this catfish.

Catfish "whiskers" help the fish find food. Close your eyes and have someone hand you different objects. Guess what each one is using only your sense of touch.

Find this heron.

Herons stand completely still while they wait for a tasty fish to swim by. Make yourself into a "statue" of a favorite animal. Have someone guess the animal.

Find the kingbird.

Kingbirds look like acrobats when they dart and twist to catch insects or defend territory. Practice your high jump, somersault, or cartwheel.

Find the water moccasin.

Water moccasins have fangs with poison in them. What are some dangerous things in your environment? Make a list of ways to stay safe.

Find this teal.

Teals spend summer in the north and fly south for the winter. On a map, mark where you live and where Tiana lives (New Orleans, Louisiana).

Match these photos of swamp animals to their partners in Mama Odie's bayou:

Aurora and Phillip bundle up for a sleigh ride through the snowy boreal forest. Boreal forests are in the far north. Most of the trees there are evergreens and have needles instead of leaves. The plants and animals in the boreal forest are adapted for long, cold winters and short summers.

Find this pine grosbeak.

These birds sometimes fly a long way in winter to find food. What is your favorite food? Is it available all year or only during certain seasons?

Find this snowy owl.

Owls have an excellent sense of hearing. Sit very still, and quietly listen for one full minute. What did you hear? Did you hear different things as time passed?

Find this marten.

Martens use their tails to keep their balance in trees. Test your balance on one leg, then the other. How does your balance change when you close your eyes?

Find this snowshoe hare.

Hares and rabbits are different animals. Hares are bigger and have bigger hind legs and ears. Think of two other animals that share traits. Draw and label them.

Find this lynx.

Lynxes and the other animals in the boreal forest are perfectly comfortable in their cold, snowy environment. What would you bring to go snow camping? Make a list.

Match these photos of boreal forest animals to their partners in the snowy scene:

It's moving day! Riley and her parents drive through the city toward their new home. In a city, people with different backgrounds and ways of life live and work together. Animals live there too—in parks, backyards, streets and alleys, and even in people's homes. Cities are found all over the world.

Find this dog.

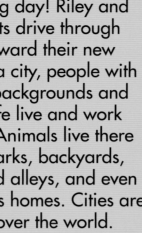

When dogs are trained, both the dogs and their people are happier. Do you or does someone you know have a pet? What helps keep the pet safe and happy?

Find this squirrel.

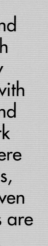

One way squirrels communicate is by flicking their tails. With a partner, see if you can have a conversation using only body language.

Find this cat.

House cats keep up their hunting skills by playing with toys or with each other. What are your favorite games? What skills do these games help you practice?

Find this finch.

Many forest and grassland birds have adapted to living in or near cities. What is something familiar to you now that used to feel new and strange?

Find this person.

The first city was established thousands of years ago. Find out how old your city, town, or village is, and how long your family has lived there.

Match these photos of city animals with their partners on Riley's street:

Stampede back to the savanna and sort the animals.

Which animals have four legs?
Which animals have two legs?
Which animals have fur?
Which animals have feathers?
Which animals do you see out in the open?
Which animals do you see in caves?

Try this!
Do you think your pace will change if you practice your sprint? Pick a start and finish line and ask someone to time you. Practice running in that same spot every other day. Use the same shoes and run at the same time each day. After two weeks, get someone to time you again. What did the practice do for your pace? Record your progress on a chart.

Sample Chart

Start: Our tree	End: Corner mailbox	
Date	Time of day	My time
May 14	3:15	20 sec
May 28	3:21	18 sec

Hike back to the temperate forest and practice plant identification.

Find leaves with these different leaf features:

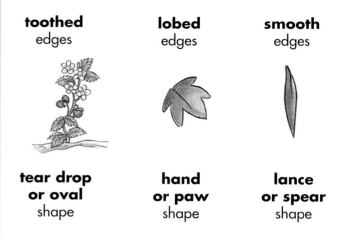

toothed edges   **lobed** edges   **smooth** edges

tear drop or oval shape   **hand or paw** shape   **lance or spear** shape

Try this!
Observe plants and trees near your home. In each case, look at the leaf edge, the leaf shape, and whether the leaf is alone on its stem or part of a group. Also look at its veins, its texture, and whether its stem is smooth, rough, or fuzzy. Make a botanist's notebook: draw the leaves and label their traits.

Wade back to the river and look for materials that animals could use to build homes.

In what ways could wood be used?

How could stones be used?

How could mud or dirt be used?

What other things in the picture could be used for animal homes?

Try this!
Do you think it's easier for salmon to swim out to sea or back to their birthplace? Outdoors or in your bathtub, place a bowl under one side of a cookie sheet so the cookie sheet sits at an angle. The lower side is the sea. The higher side is the salmons' birthplace. Slowly pour water on the higher side to form a "river" flowing down the tray. In which direction would it be easier to swim?

Swim back to the reef and find the coral. Why do you think these each have the names they do?

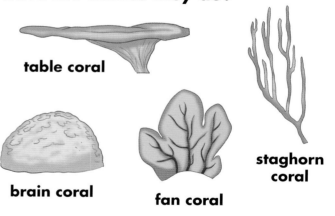

table coral

brain coral   fan coral

staghorn coral

Try this!
In real life, some of Dory's ocean friends are *endangered*—not very many of them are left. But there are people dedicated to helping endangered animal populations grow healthy again. You can help too. Ask your zoo or park service about an endangered species in your area and what you can do to help. You might restore a habitat, do "citizen science" observations, or collect money to donate.

Climb back to the tepui and find animals that have these useful traits:

webbed back feet to help it swim

a flashy, colorful head-crest to attract a mate

big front claws to help it dig

coloring that helps it blend in

big wings that help it stay warm and help it fly

Try this!
The tepuis were formed when soft parts of a giant rock *eroded*, or wore down, and left only the hardest parts still standing high. See how this type of erosion works: Cover a rock in sand or flour so you can't see it. Slowly pour water over your mountain. Watch the softer part wear down to expose the harder rock.

Row back to the swamp to look and count.

How many types of birds do you see? To tell them apart, pay attention to the different shaped beaks.

How many types of fish do you see? To tell them apart, pay attention to the different shaped mouths and fins.

How many types of plants do you see growing in the water? To tell them apart, pay attention to the different shaped leaves.

Try this!
On your map that shows where you live and where Tiana lives, use a new color to mark places you have visited. Mark places you want to visit with another color. Now find the map's legend. It will tell you how to read distance on the map. Choose one of the places you marked. What is the distance between where you live and that place? Which mark is farthest from your home? Which is closest?

Snowshoe back to the boreal forest and find animals based on the kind of lunch they're looking for.

The animals below eat mostly plant parts, such as greens, seeds, berries, and bark. (Some of them like insects.)

hares
songbirds
squirrels   **rabbit** **vole**

The animals below are predators. That means they mainly eat other critters.

lynx
martens
owls  **fox** **ermine**

Try this!
Lynxes have huge, furry paws with toes that spread wide. Like snowshoes, their paws keep them from sinking into the snow when they walk. Put a circular piece of cardboard and a long thin piece of cardboard in a pan of water. Place pennies one at a time on each piece. Does the wider piece or the narrower piece hold more weight before sinking?

Rush back to the city and look for different ways we humans adapt to our environment.

How many types of transportation can you find?

How many methods of getting something to eat do you see?

How many people are ready for cool weather?

How many people are ready for sunny weather?

How many ways do you see people communicating?

Try this!
Get permission from a trusted adult to interview someone in your community. Ask them how long they've lived in the neighborhood. Did they spend their childhood here or move in after they were grown up? How have things changed over time? What is their favorite thing to do in the neighborhood? What is your favorite thing?